MY FIRST

1000

ENGLISH-ESPAÑOL WORDS

Translated by: Marcela Riomalo

Wonder House

abecedario (alphabet)

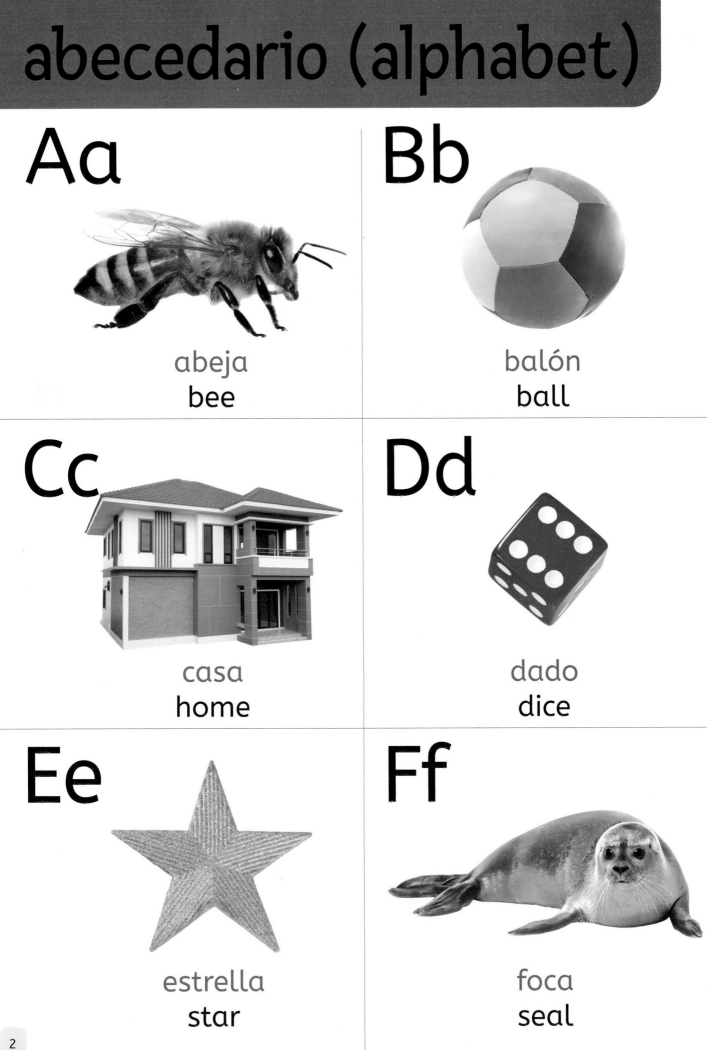

Aa

abeja
bee

Bb

balón
ball

Cc

casa
home

Dd

dado
dice

Ee

estrella
star

Ff

foca
seal

Gg

gato
cat

Hh

huevo
egg

Ii

iglú
igloo

Jj

jarra
jug

Kk

kimono
kimono

Ll

limón
lemon

Mm

mono
monkey

Nn

nido
nest

Oo

oliva
olive

Pp

pan
bread

Qq

queso
cheese

Rr

rosa
rose

Ss

saco
bag

Tt

tambor
drum

Uu

uva
grape

Vv

volcán
volcano

Ww

waffle
waffle

Xx

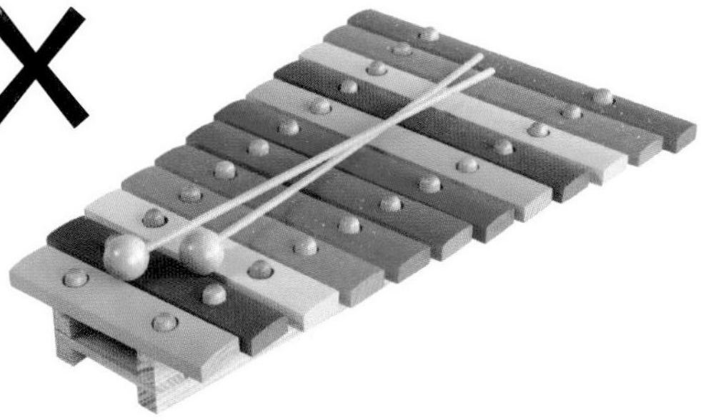

xylófono
xylophone

Yy

yate
yatch

Zz

zapatos
shoes

números (numbers)

1 uno
one

2 dos
two

3 tres
three

4 cuatro
four

5 cinco
five
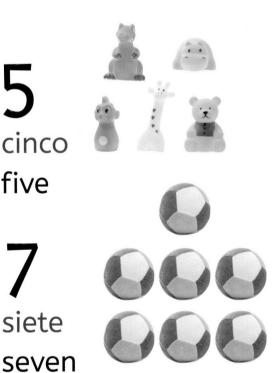

6 seis
six

7 siete
seven

8 ocho
eight

9 nueve
nine

10 diez
ten

11
once
eleven

12
doce
twelve

13
trece
thirteen

14
catorce
fourteen

15
quince
fifteen

16
dieciséis
sixteen

17
diecisiete
seventeen

18
dieciocho
eighteen

19
diecinueve
nineteen

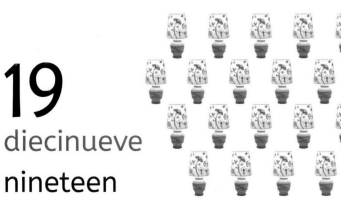

20
veinte
twenty

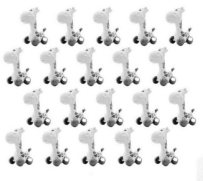

colores (colors)

rojo
red

cardenal
cardinal

verde
green

cactus
cactus

azul
blue

zafiro
sapphire

amarillo
yellow

limón
lemon

naranja
orange

polo
ice candy

violeta
violet

lilas
lilac

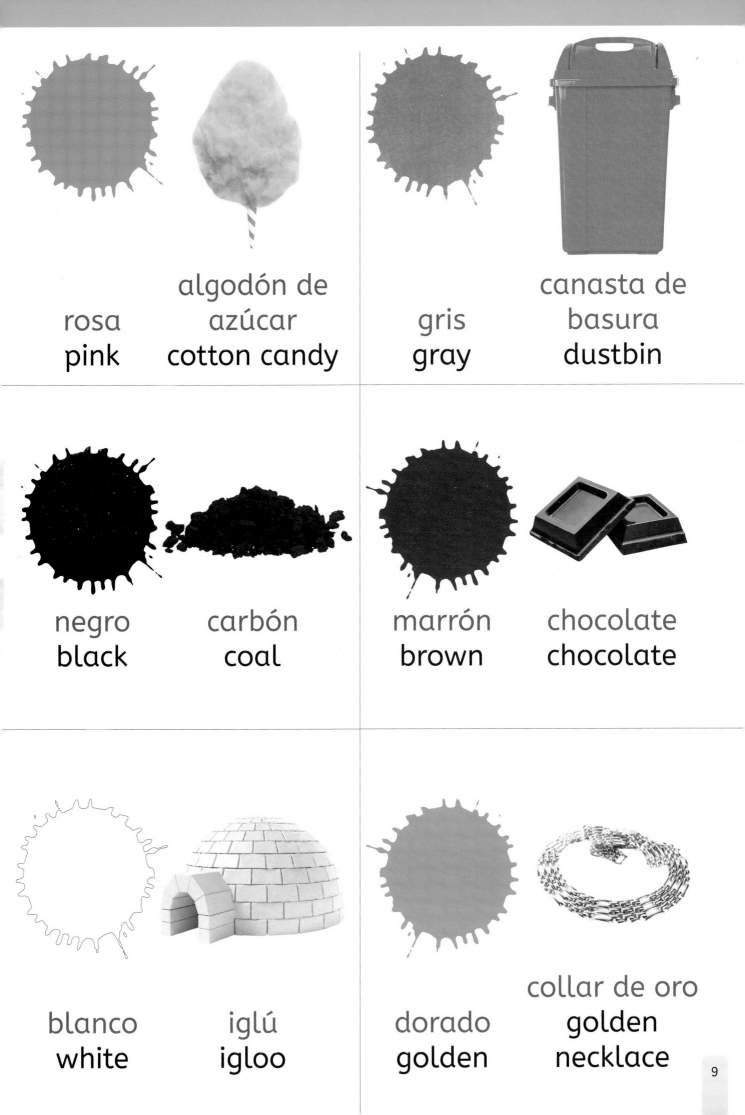

rosa
pink

algodón de azúcar
cotton candy

gris
gray

canasta de basura
dustbin

negro
black

carbón
coal

marrón
brown

chocolate
chocolate

blanco
white

iglú
igloo

dorado
golden

collar de oro
golden necklace

figuras (shapes)

círculo
circle

rueda
wheel

botón
button

cuadrado
square

galleta
cracker

tablero de ajedrez
chessboard

rectángulo
rectangle

sobre de papel
envelope

naipe
playing card

triángulo
triangle

sándwich
sandwich

escuadra
traffic sign

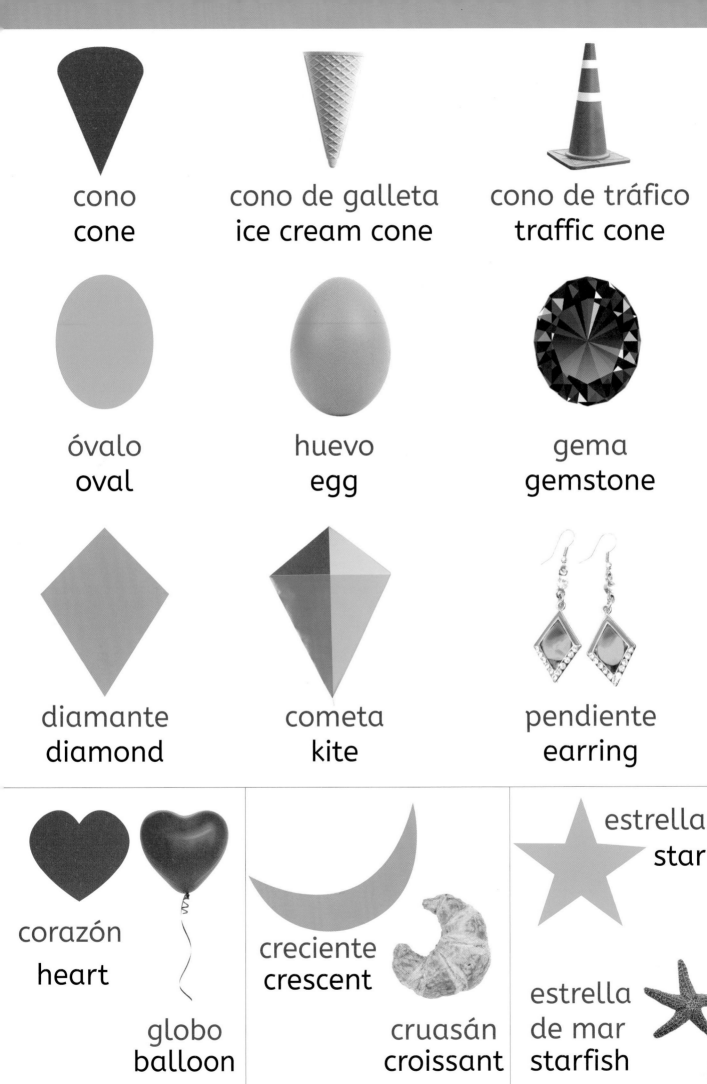

cono
cone

cono de galleta
ice cream cone

cono de tráfico
traffic cone

óvalo
oval

huevo
egg

gema
gemstone

diamante
diamond

cometa
kite

pendiente
earring

corazón
heart

globo
balloon

creciente
crescent

cruasán
croissant

estrella
star

estrella
de mar
starfish

opuestos (opposites)

lento **slow**	rápido **fast**	poco **few**	mucho **many**
caliente **hot**	frío **cold**	suave **soft**	duro **hard**
delante **front**	detrás **back**	dentro **inside**	fuera **outside**

vacío **empty**	lleno **full**	sucio **dirty**	limpio **clean**
grande **big**	pequeño **small**	pesado **heavy**	liviano **light**
abierto **open**	cerrado **closed**	feliz **happy**	triste **sad**
áspero **rough**	suave **smooth**	viejo **old**	nuevo **new**

frutas (fruits)

manzana apple	naranja orange	sandía watermelon	coco coconut
plátano banana	piña pineapple	durazno peach	mango mango
melón cantaloupe	papaya papaya	cereza cherry	pera pear
uva grape	granada pomegranate	kiwi kiwi	aguacate avocado

dátil
date

fresa
strawberry

toronja
grapefruit

higo
fig

guayaba
guava

arándano azul
blueberry

albaricoque
apricot

pitaya
dragon fruit

chirimoya
custard apple

frambuesa
raspberry

mora
blackberry

fruta estrella
starfruit

ciruela
plum

arándano rojo
cranberry

lychee
litchi

grosella
gooseberry

15

vegetales (vegetables)

coliflor	col	pimiento verde	zanahoria
cauliflower	**cabbage**	**green bell pepper**	**carrot**

calabaza	calabacín	espinaca	maíz
pumpkin	**zucchini**	**spinach**	**corn**

ocra	lechuga	puerro	rábano
okra	**lettuce**	**leek**	**radish**

cebolla	nabo	patata	patata dulce
onion	**turnip**	**potato**	**sweet potato**

calabaza
amarga
bitter gourd

**fríjol francés
french bean**

brócoli
broccoli

col
rizada
kale

remolacha
beetroot

arveja
green pea

berenjena
eggplant

cebolleta
**spring
onion**

yuca
yam

alcachofa
artichoke

calabaza
vinatera
**bottle
gourd**

jengibre
ginger

ajo
garlic

pepino
cohombro
cucumber

espárrago
asparagus

apio
celery

comida (food)

leche
milk

sushi
sushi

ensalada
salad

tofu
tofu

taco
taco

cornflakes
cornflakes

sopa
soup

helado
ice cream

zumo
juice

waffle
waffle

pez
fish

pollo
chicken

tarta
pie

camarones
shrimp

arroz
rice

cereales
cereal

champiñón
mushroom

queso
cheese

frutos secos
trail mix

pasta
pasta

yogurt
yogurt

pancake
pancake

macarrón
macaroni

pizza
pizza

galleta
cookie

madalena
muffin

mantequilla
butter

pan
bread

hummus
hummus

miel
honey

noodles
oatmeal

palomitas
de maíz
popcorn

transporte (transport)

bicicleta
bicycle

tandem
tandem

tabla de skate
skateboard

uniciclo
unicycle

moto
scooter

motocicleta
motorcycle

auto
car

taxi
taxi

van
van

auto
de carrera
go-cart

auto
de nieve
snowmobile

auto
de golf
golf cart

autobús
bus

trailer
lorry

camión
de basura
garbage truck

camión de
bomberos
fire engine

camión
truck

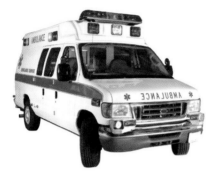

ambulancia
ambulance

tractor
tractor

grúa
tow truck

camión
de comida
food wagon

excavadora
digger

camión
de petróleo
oil tanker

caravana
caravan

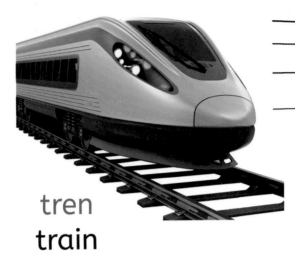

tren
train

teleférico
cable car

tranvía
tram

avión
airplane

globo
**hot-air
balloon**

helicóptero
helicopter

dirigible
blimp

cohete
rocket

nave espacial
space shuttle

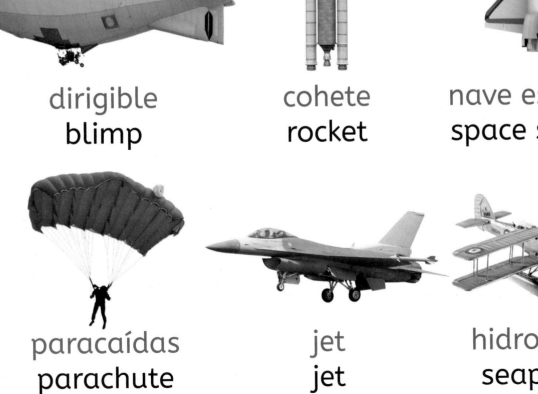

paracaídas
parachute

jet
jet

hidroavión
seaplane

bote de pesca
fishing boat

kayak
kayak

yate
yacht

ferry
ferry

jet ski
jet ski

raft
raft

barco de carga
cargo ship

velero
sailboat

bote
boat

barco
ship

submarino
submarine

aerodeslizador
hovercraft

profesiones (professions)

panadero
baker

chef
chef

detective
detective

abogada
lawyer

doctora
doctor

oficial de
policía
police
officer

maestro
teacher

granjero
farmer

mecánico
mechanic

soldado
soldier

músico
musician

bombero
firefighter

carpintero
carpenter

florista
florist

astronauta
astronaut

científico
scientist

arquitecta
architect

cartero
delivery
person

fotógrafa
photographer

piloto
pilot

peluquera
hairdresser

artista
artist

aves (birds)

loro
parrot

pavo real
peacock

búho
owl

cisne
swan

pájaro
carpintero
woodpecker

martín
pescador
kingfisher

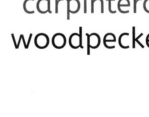

cuervo
crow

gorrión
sparrow

paloma
pigeon

pingüino
penguin

buitre
vulture

águila
eagle

flamenco
flamingo

pinzón cebra
zebra finch

avestruz
ostrich

grua
crane

frailecillo
puffin

colibrí
hummingbird

miná
mynah

petirrojo
robin

tucán
toucan

cálao
hornbill

mascotas y animales de granja (pets & farm animals)

| perro | gato | oveja | conejo |
| dog | cat | sheep | rabbit |

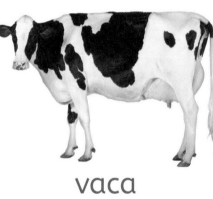

| cabra | vaca | toro |
| goat | cow | bull |

| caballo | camello | llama |
| horse | camel | llama |

yak
yak

burro
donkey

gallina
hen

búfalo
buffalo

alpaca
alpaca

emú
emu

gallo
rooster

hurón
ferret

conejillo
de indias
guinea pig

hámster
hamster

pato
duck

ganso
goose

pavo
turkey

animales salvajes (wild animals)

tigre
tiger

león
lion

jirafa
giraffe

cebra
zebra

lobo
wolf

canguro
kangaroo

ciervo
deer

zorro
fox

oso
bear

oso polar
polar bear

rinoceronte
rhinoceros

chita
cheetah

hipopótamo
hippopotamus

oso panda
panda

elefante
elephant

mono
monkey

hiena
hyena

jabalí
boar

gorila
gorilla

puercoespín
porcupine

camaleón
chameleon

cocodrilo
crocodile

koala
koala

lémur
lemur

animales bebés (baby animals)

perro cachorro	gatito	ternero	potro de caballo
puppy	**kitten**	**cow calf**	**horse foal**

león cachorro	tigre cachorro	polluelo	patito
lion cub	**tiger cub**	**chick**	**duckling**

cervatillo	potro de burro	cría de jirafa	potro de cebra
deer fawn	**donkey foal**	**giraffe calf**	**zebra foal**

pingüino polluelo
penguin chick

cordero
lamb

oso cachorro
bear cub

conejillo
kit

cabrita
kid

búho bebé
owlet

loro
polluelo
parrot chick

elefante
cachorro
elephant calf

rinoceronte
cachorro
rhinoceros calf

tortuga bebé
baby tortoise

oso polar
cachorro
polar bear cub

cisne bebé
swan cygnet

animales marinos (sea animals)

pez payaso
clownfish

pez ángel
angelfish

pez globo
balloonfish

ballena
pilot whale

delfín
dolphin

medusa
jellyfish

tortuga marina
sea turtle

tiburón
shark

**caballo
de mar**
seahorse

anguila
eel

pez espada
swordfish

almeja
clam

morsa
walrus

foca
seal

nautilo
nautilus

atún
tuna

mantarraya
stingray

ostra
oyster

pulpo
octopus

calamar
squid

langosta
lobster

palometa
pomfret

coral
coral

cangrejo
crab

insectos (insects)

hormiga
ant

mariposa
butterfly

mosquito
mosquito

abeja
bee

polilla
moth

grillo
grasshopper

amatista
stick insect

libélula
dragonfly

escarabajo
beetle

escorpión
scorpion

araña
spider

caracol
snail

mi cuerpo (my body)

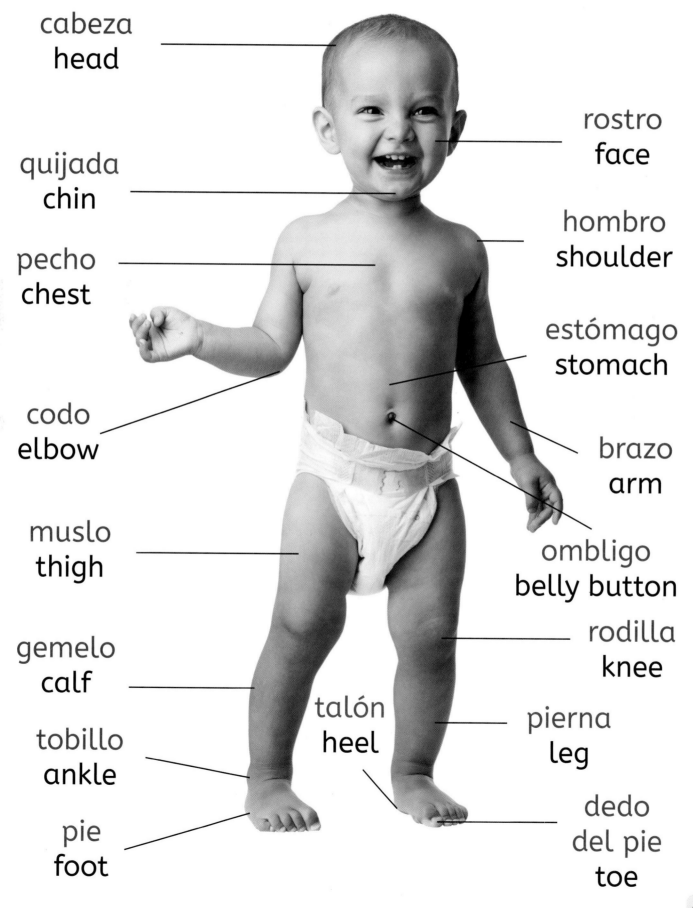

cabeza
head

rostro
face

quijada
chin

hombro
shoulder

pecho
chest

estómago
stomach

codo
elbow

brazo
arm

muslo
thigh

ombligo
belly button

gemelo
calf

rodilla
knee

talón
heel

pierna
leg

tobillo
ankle

pie
foot

dedo
del pie
toe

mi rostro (my face)

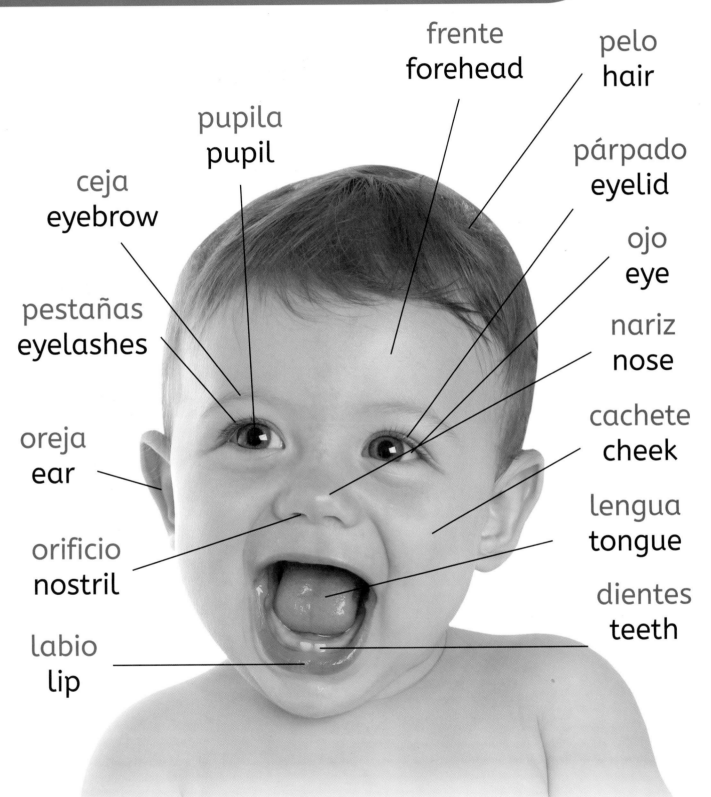

frente
forehead

pelo
hair

pupila
pupil

párpado
eyelid

ceja
eyebrow

ojo
eye

nariz
nose

pestañas
eyelashes

cachete
cheek

oreja
ear

lengua
tongue

orificio
nostril

dientes
teeth

labio
lip

mis manos (my hands)

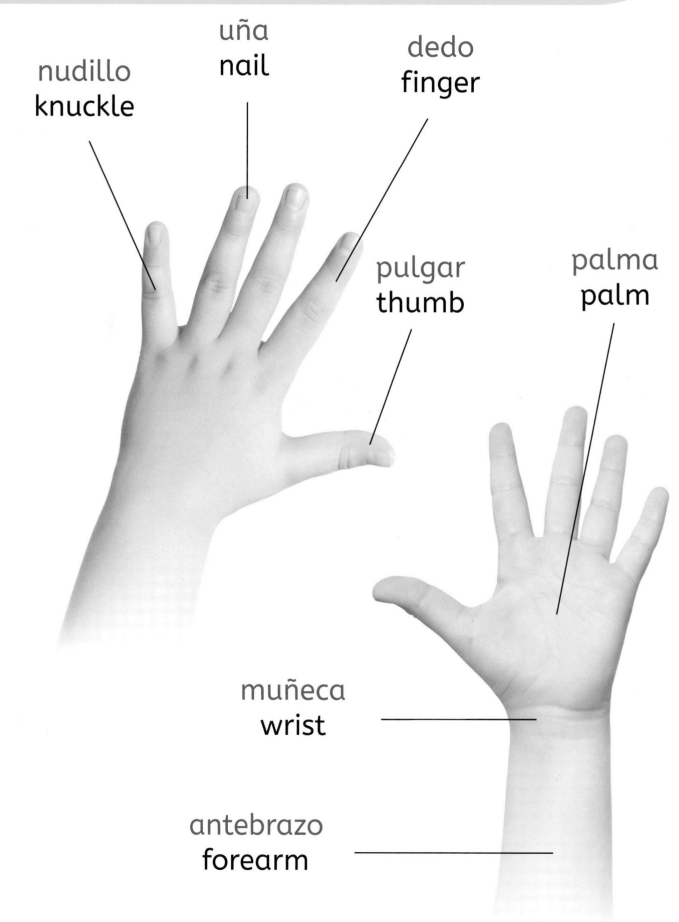

nudillo
knuckle

uña
nail

dedo
finger

pulgar
thumb

palma
palm

muñeca
wrist

antebrazo
forearm

caras de bebé (baby faces)

riendo
laughing

llorando
crying

sonriendo
smiling

sorprendido
surprised

emocionada
excited

pensando
thinking

bostezando
yawning

preocupado
worried

asustado
scared

mis sentidos (my senses)

tacto
touch

vista
sight

oído
hear

olfato
smell

gusto
taste

juguetes (toys)

carrito
toy car

maraca
rattle

dinosaurio
dinosaur

juguete de baño
bath toy

damas chinas
chinese checkers

top
top

casa de muñecas
dollhouse

cubo rubik
rubik's cube

robot
robot

set de
tren
train set

caballito de
madera
rocking horse

lazo para
saltar
skipping rope

triciclo
tricycle

bloques
blocks

set de cocina
kitchen set

títeres
de dedo
finger puppet

máscara
mask

teléfono
de juguete
toy phone

juguete
blando
soft toy

anillos
apilables
ring stacker

set de
doctor
doctor set

rompecabezas
jigsaw puzzle

teclado
de música
musical keyboard

canicas
marble

túnel de juguete
toy tunnel

juguete de halar
push-along toy

set de bolos
bowling set

laberinto
labyrinth

juguete
tambaleante
tumbler

ábaco
abacus

anillos
para arrojar
ring toss

molinillo
pinwheel

auto a
control remoto
**remote
control car**

tablero
mágico
magic board

aro de
cintura
hula hoop

juguete
de aplausos
toy car

bloques de
construcción
building blocks

triqui
tic-tac-toe

tapete
de juego
play mat

muñeca
doll

juguete
de figuras
shape sorter

frisbee
frisbee

yo-yo
yo-yo

micrófono
microphone

caja de
juguetes
toy storage box

bola espacial
**space hopper
ball**

objetos de bebe (baby objects)

babero
bib

chupete
sipper

silla alta
high chair

tetero
milk bottle

manta
blanket

cuna
crib

caminador
walker

coche
stroller

balón
ball

zapatos
shoes

bacinilla
potty seat

bañera
bath tub

mecedora
baby rocker

silla de coche
car seat

peineta
comb

cuchara
spoon

mameluco
romper

tazón
bowl

**almohada
para bebé**
baby pillow

mosquitero
mosquito net

maleta
bag

aceite
para bebé
baby oil

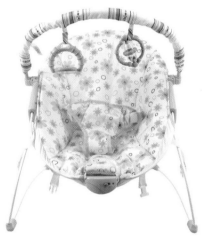

saltarín
para bebé
baby bouncer

juguete
para dientes
teether

talco
para bebé
baby powder

móvil
cot mobile

cepillo
de dientes
toothbrush

botines
booties

vestidor
dresser

mitones
mitten

moisés
bassinet

cargador de bebé
baby carrier

crayola
crayon

comida
de bebé
baby food

colchón
mattress

portarretrato
photo frame

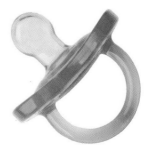

chupo
pacifier

salón (living room)

cojín
cushion

sofá
sofa

sillón
armchair

mesa
de centro
center table

tapete
carpet

cortina
curtain

televisor
television

reloj de pared
wall clock

teléfono
telephone

chimenea
fireplace

lámpara
de techo
hanging light

aire
acondicionado
air conditioner

jarrón
vase

habitación (bedroom)

duvet
duvet

almohada
pillow

cama
bed

armario
wardrobe

tocador
dressing table

puff
bean bag

radio
radio

tapete de
entrada
doormat

reloj
de alarma
alarm clock

ventana
window

lámpara
de mesa
table lamp

ventilador
fan

mesa para
planchar
ironing board

cómoda
chest of
drawers

baño (bathroom)

jabonera
soap dish

gabinete
cabinet

enjuague bucal
mouth freshener

ducha
shower

canasta de
ropa sucia
laundry hamper

cisterna
toilet pot

lavamanos
washbasin

esponja
vegetal
loofah

taza
mug

papel
de baño
toilet paper

espejo
mirror

cepillo
de baño
bath brush

cepillo
del pelo
hairbrush

pasta dental
toothpaste

champú
shampoo

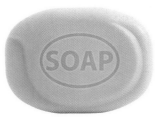

jabón
soap

toalla
towel

pañuelo de papel
tissue paper

persiana
blinds

extractor
exhaust fan

aceite del pelo
hair oil

esponja
sponge

lavadora
washing machine

detergente
washing powder

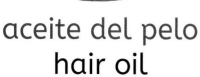

bastoncillo de algodón
cotton swab

secador de pelo
hair dryer

cocina (kitchen)

estufa
de gas
gas stove

encendedor
de gas
gas lighter

chimenea
chimney

tabla para cortar
chopping board

espátula
spatula

plato
plate

rodillo
rolling pin

olla a presión
pressure cooker

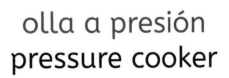

cubiertos
cutlery

bandeja
tray

jarra
jar

vaso
glass

lavaplatos
sink

lavaplatos eléctrico
dishwasher

refrigerador
refrigerator

microondas
microwave oven

taza
cup

plato para taza
saucer

olla
saucepan

delantal
apron

toalla pequeña
tea towel

sartén
frying pan

parrilla
grill

cafetera
coffee maker

batidor
whisk

licuadora
blender

tetera
kettle

tostadora
toaster

jardín (garden)

pasto
grass

grama
hedge

hojas
leaves

rodillo de miel
honeycomb

nido
nest

árbol
tree

palos
sticks

oruga
caterpillar

lombriz
de tierra
earthworm

manguera
garden hose

regadera
watering can

invernadero
greenhouse

pajarera
birdhouse

horqueta
garden fork

rastrillo
rake

mariquita
ladybug

avispa
wasp

cortacésped
lawnmower

canasta de desechos
waste bin

semillas
seeds

pala
spade

carretilla
wheelbarrow

ladrillos
bricks

perrera
kennel

rociador
sprinkle

paleta
trowel

maceta
flowerpot

57

escuela (school)

libro
book

tiza
chalk

tablero
negro
blackboard

estudiantes
students

marcador
marker

tablero
blanco
whiteboard

escritorio
desk

lámpara
lamp

plastilina
clay

corrector
líquido
pen corrector

dibujo
drawing

caballete
easel

cuaderno
notebook

lápiz
pencil

calculadora
calculator

borrador
eraser

regla
ruler

quitapolvo
duster

resaltador
felt tip pen

acuarela
watercolor

pincel
brush

corcho
softboard

globo
globe

escarapela
badge

pegante
glue

chinche
tack

computador
computer

papelera
waste bin

acuario
aquarium

calendario
calendar

papel
paper

parque (park)

banca
bench

tiovivo
merry-go-round

rodadero
slide

subibaja
see-saw

columpio
swing

arenera
sandpit

canasta
de picnic
picnic basket

niños
children

fuente
fountain

cama
de flores
flower bed

patines
roller skates

farol
lamp post

coche
pushchair

portón
gate

reja
fence

pasamanos
monkey bars

camino
path

árbol
tree

casa de juegos
playhouse

gimnasio
tipo selva
jungle gym

estatua
statue

deportes (sports)

ciclismo
cycling

cricket
cricket

hockey
hockey

béisbol
baseball

basquetbol
basketball

ping-pong
table tennis

ajedrez
chess

tiro al arco
archery

gimnasia
gymnastics

judo
judo

fútbol
football

rugby
rugby

tennis
tennis

bádminton
badminton

patinaje
en hielo
ice skating

golf
golf

camping (camping)

mochila
backpack

kit de primeros auxilios
first aid kit

botella de agua
water bottle

bolsa de dormir
sleeping bag

tienda de campaña
tent

mapa
map

batería
battery

linterna
torch

farol
lantern

brújula
compass

termo
thermos

botas
de montaña
hiking boots

estufa de
campaña
camping stove

encendedor
lighter

cámara
de fotos
camera

binoculares
binoculars

cámara
de video
video camera

playa (seaside)

sombrero
hat

lentes de sol
sunglasses

castillo
de arena
sandcastle

sombrilla
umbrella

flotador
swimming ring

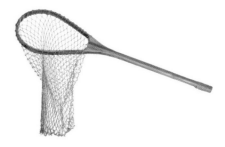

red de pesca
fishing net

bandera
flag

traje de buceo
diving suit

máscara
de buceo
diving mask

aletas
flippers

bloqueador solar
sunscreen

traje de baño
swimsuit

isla
island

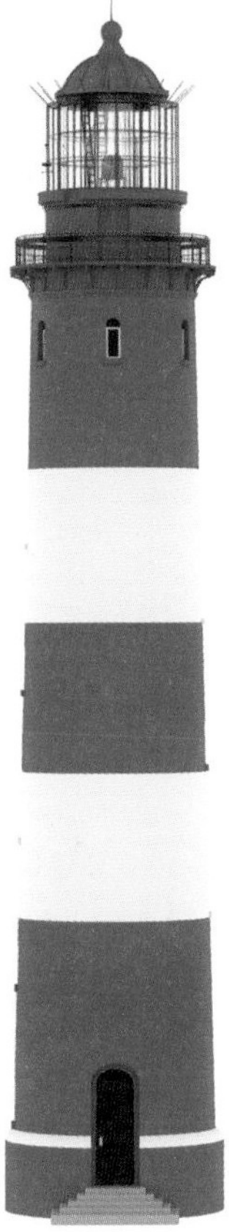

tabla
de surf
surfboard

juguetes
de playa
beach toys

faro
lighthouse

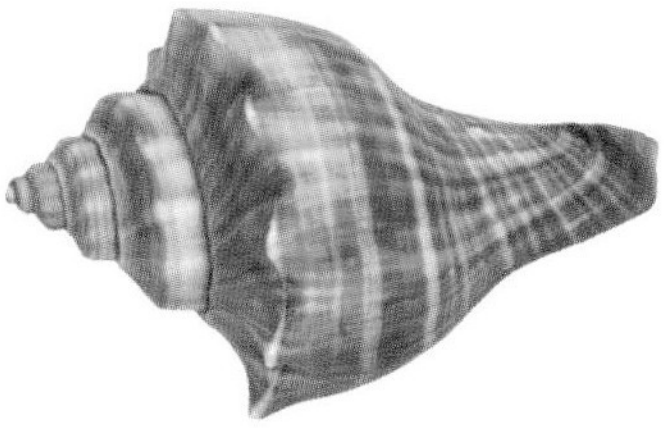

soga
rope

alga
seaweed

concha
shell

piedrecillas
pebbles

gaviota
seagull

tapete de
gimnasia
mat

ropa (clothes)

chal
shawl

pantalones cortos
shorts

guantes
gloves

bufanda
scarf

chaqueta
jacket

sudadera
sweatshirt

vestido
de noche
night dress

pijama
pyjamas

camiseta
t-shirt

camisa
shirt

falda
skirt

calcetines
socks

saco
sweater

cárdigan
cardigan

vestido
de gala
gown

pantalones
trousers

chompa
raincoat

mono
overalls

gorro
de lana
woolen cap

vaqueros
jeans

traje
suit

blazer
blazer

corbata
tie

abrigo
coat

fiesta (party)

lentes de fiesta
party glasses

antifaz
party mask

bebida helada
cold drink

cenefa
paper chain

pompas de jabón
party popper

polo
popsicle

gorro de fiesta
party hat

oso de peluche
teddy bear

vestido de fiesta
party dress

regalos
gifts

bombilla
lightbulb

granizado
slush

rosquillas
donuts

pudín de chocolate
chocolate pudding

mantel
tablecloth

lazo
ribbon

corona
tiara

pajita
straw

vela
candle

circo (circus)

aro
hoop

payaso
clown

maestro
de aros
ringmaster

sombrero
de payaso
clown's cap

carpa
de circo
circus tent

malabarismo
juggling

corbatín
de payaso
clown's bow

acrobacia
acrobatics

trapecio
trapeze

varita
mágica
magic stick

escalera
de cuerda
rope ladder

nariz roja
red nose

sombrero
de mago
**magician's
hat**

pintura de rostro
face paint

mago
magician

personajes y objetos de cuento (words in a story)

hada
fairy

reina
queen

corona
crown

rey
king

princesa
princess

príncipe
prince

castillo
castle

guerrero
warrior

espada
sword

escudo
shield

arco
bow

flecha
arrow

unicornio
unicorn

caballero
knight

pirata
pirate

tesoro
treasure

mago
wizard

escoba
broomstick

bruja
witch

vampiro
vampire

monstruo
monster

dragón
dragon

sirena
mermaid

varita
wand

verbos (action words)

reír
laugh

sonreír
smile

comer
eat

beber
drink

leer
read

jugar
play

hablar
talk

escribir
write

enfurecerse
angry

llorar
cry

gatear
crawl

escalar
climb

caminar
walk

agarrar
catch

lanzar
throw

tomar
pick

dormir
sleep

limpiar
wash

doblarse
bend

halar
pull

pintar
paint

pensar
think

escuchar
listen

bailar
dance

esconder
hide

arrodillarse
kneel

cortar
cut

barrer
sweep

cantar
sing

correr
run

patear
kick

cargar
carry

flores (flowers)

girasol
sunflower

caléndula
marigold

iris
iris

lotus
lotus

tulipán
tulip

clavel
carnation

lila
lily

lirio
canna

jasmín
jasmine

pensamiento
pansy

rosa
rose

margarita
daisy

narciso
daffodil

jacinto
hyacinth

bígaro
periwinkle

zinnia
zinnia

dalia
dahlia

amapola
poppy

petunia
petunia

orquídea
orchid

bella de día
morning glory

hibisco
hibiscus

buganvilia
bougainvillea

ranúnculo
buttercup

instrumentos musicales (musical instruments)

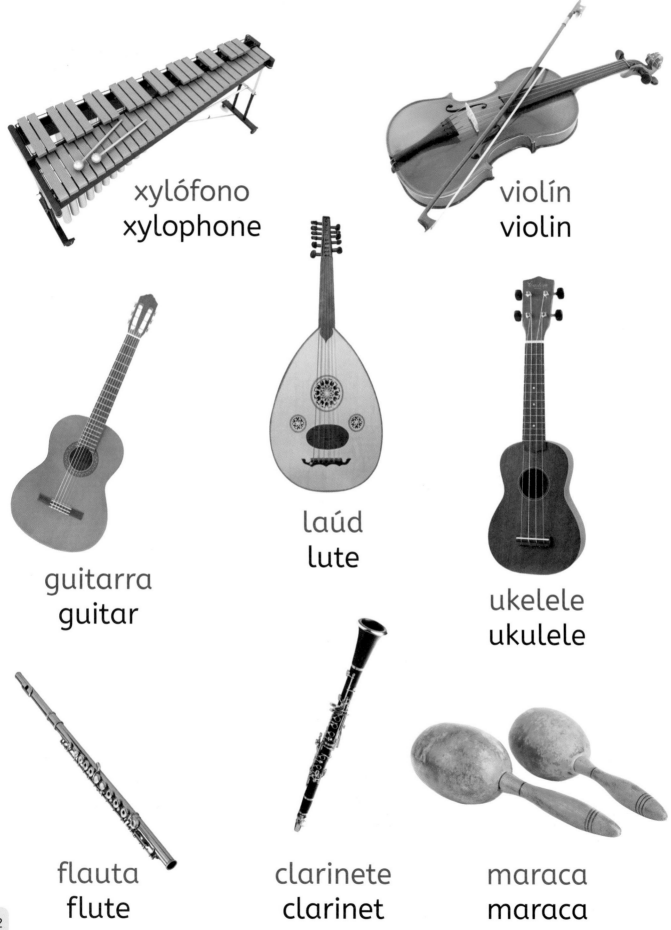

xylófono
xylophone

violín
violin

guitarra
guitar

laúd
lute

ukelele
ukulele

flauta
flute

clarinete
clarinet

maraca
maraca

piano
piano

sintetizador
synthesizer

platillo
cymbal

triángulo
triangle

flauta dulce
recorder

mandolina
mandolin

bongo
bongo drum

tambor
drum

gong
gong

tabla
tabla

harpa
harp

cítara
sitar

harmonio
harmonium

pandereta
tambourine

dhol
dhol

harmónica
harmonica

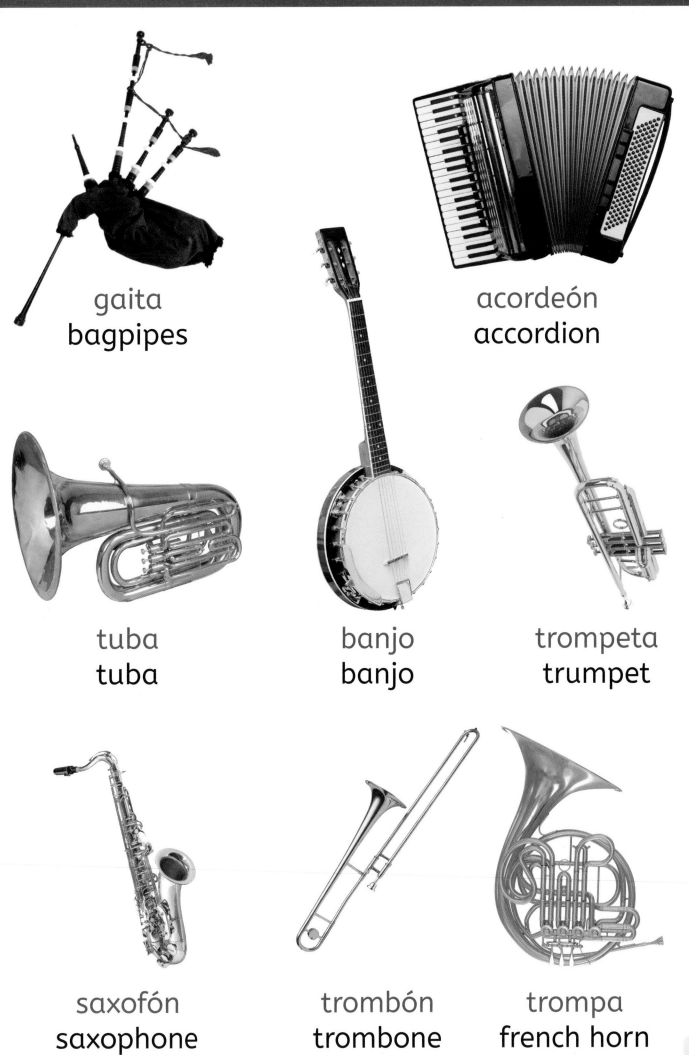

gaita
bagpipes

acordeón
accordion

tuba
tuba

banjo
banjo

trompeta
trumpet

saxofón
saxophone

trombón
trombone

trompa
french horn

hospital (hospital)

enfermero
nurse

paciente
patient

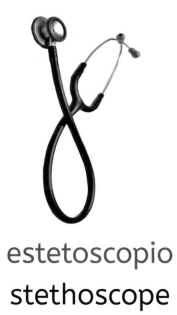

estetoscopio
stethoscope

doctora
doctor

banditas plásticas
sticking plaster

vendaje
bandage

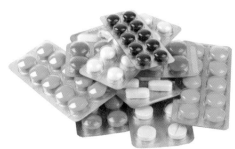

medicina
medicine

remedio
syrup

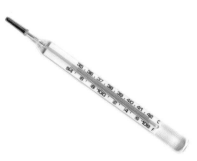

termómetro
thermometer

caminador
walking stick

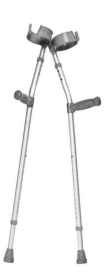

muletas
crutches

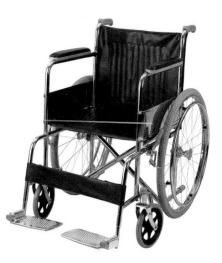

silla de ruedas
wheelchair

camilla
hospital bed

guantes quirúrgicos
medical gloves

mascarilla
surgical mask

yeso
plaster

extensor
stretcher

bandeja médica
medical tray

accesorios (accessories)

anillo
ring

horquilla de pelo
hair clips

pendientes
earring

diadema
hairband

llavero
key chain

reloj
wrist watch

corbatín
bowtie

brazalete
bracelet

bolso
purse

estuche
clutch

cinturón
belt